Ladies, The Writing Is On The Wall

Why Men Do the Things They Do, When Allowed?

Many books have been written on how a woman should act and think but fail to encompass the fact that every woman enters a relationship for various reasons.

Adrian Weber

authorHOUSE®

AuthorHouse™
1663 Liberty Drive
Bloomington, IN 47403
www.authorhouse.com
Phone: 1-800-839-8640

First published by AuthorHouse 1/19/2010

ISBN: 978-1-4490-7660-3 (e)
ISBN: 978-1-4490-7659-7 (sc)
ISBN: 978-1-4490-7658-0 (hc)

Library of Congress Control Number: 2010900770

Printed in the United States of America
Bloomington, Indiana

This book is printed on acid-free paper.

Table of Contents

Acknowledgments

When I first started this project, I often concerned myself with how practical and informative my work would be. I wrote this book so that it may be thought provoking while having a positive impact on my readers and their current relationships. I wanted to know if my material would be helpful and practical enough for my readers to refer to in the times prior to entering a potential relationship. I hope to have accomplished as much.

With that being said, I would like to extend my heartfelt thanks to the many women and men who shared with me their experiences of successful as well as failed relationships. For without them this book would not be possible. I would also like to thank my dear friend and mentor Justinah McFadden for her encouragement and diligence in keeping me on the writer's path. Justinah McFadden is an accomplished writer, poet and novelist with five published works and a fifth in progress. Her inspiring words motivated me to write on a daily basis until my project was completed. Without her constructive criticisms, this book would lack the pertinent information conducive to having a fulfilling relationship. For this I will always be grateful.

About the Author

First time author **Adrian Weber** has touched the world of book writing with his first release, *"Ladies, The Writing is on The Wall."* When he first presented this idea he received an overwhelming response, prompting him to take on this project. During his professional career in law enforcement Adrian has witnessed many hardships that women endured over the years. With compassion and empathy he conveys his ideologies, in the matters of love, intimacy, and what a woman should feel while being in a healthy relationship. His profound insight has helped both men and women to achieve both fulfilling and long lasting relationships. Adrian speaks candidly about issues that affect us all. This writer is on his way to being highly recognized as a valuable source of practical and thought provoking wisdom.

Cover design by: Kyle Daniel Charles
Illustrations by: Kyle Daniel Charles

Preface

I would like to begin by letting my readers know that this material is in direct response to the misinformation contained in the many books being distributed when it comes to matters involving love, intimacy and relationships. This often biased information is based on the authors' opinions alone. I thought, no better yet, I felt obligated to write a book in response to these books and clarify in detail what it is a man expects as well as what a woman should expect while being a relationship. More importantly, I reveal how a man views the circumstances he encounters during a relationship and how to make the distinction as to whether or not a man *loves you* or is *in love with you*. I think the explanation will surprise you and at minimum prompt you to analyze your current or past relationships. This is a no-nonsense, straight-to-the-point kind of reading which we all can appreciate and relate to. This will be the book that you refer to time and time again to help you decipher what it is he really feels and thinks. The difference is in this book, I don't just write about my own experiences, I also write about the experiences of others and how they dealt with the circumstances they encountered. I then give an analytical synopsis of what went wrong and how the situation could have possibly been avoided. In addition, I give actual accounts of similar circumstances given by anonymous women.

While reading *"Ladies, The Writing Is On The Wall"* you will see why these archaic ideologies given in recent releases (books) are ineffective. I will also explain why telling/making your significant other (to) wait three months before being physically intimate with him spells disaster. A man that gives his significant other a title (girlfriend, fiancée, etc.) does not necessarily indicate that he loves you. Many men use titles to inform other men in close proximity that you are spoken for. Titles are often given by men to extend courtesy to either you, family members or close friends so that you do not feel out of place or uncomfortable. It is his responses to your questions and concerns that reveal what his true intentions really are. How does he treat you when you alone with him? Does he respect you and listen to your concerns or does he just brush you off? Over a four month period, I've interviewed over one hundred men and quite a few women. The questions asked during these interviews range from various theories on relationships, what was learned, and more importantly, what was noticed while being courted for a relationship that would otherwise indicate incompatibility.

The men and women that I had the privilege of interviewing had a lot to say about how women should think and the actions that should have been taken. These men and women are from various cultures, backgrounds and nationalities. Doctors, lawyers, nurses and teachers as well as many other professionals opened up to me and expressed their thoughts and opinions on the issues involving relationships, love and intimacy. In my work I simply felt that much clarification was needed due to the misinformation as well as the lack of information given in other books I've read concerning matters of the heart.

First off I would like to disclose to my readers that I have no specialized training in matters involving relationships or matters of intimacy. I speak from experience and share with you the experiences of others. They say experience is the best teacher. There is much truth in that maxim. I do however hold certifications in the different methods of Interview and Interrogation which enables me to read the body language of people without them even being aware they are being read. What does this have to do with relationships you might ask? A whole lot, if you know what to look for. Once you know the characteristics and signs of what to look for and how to become a better listener, you will be able to make an informed decision as to whether or not you two are compatible. The material in this book will also improve your listening skills for when and how he answers the questions being asked of him. I also have actual accounts of people I have either known, been referred to or continue to remain in contact with over the years. They say this information will be thought provoking and valued by many. They were more than happy to share their stories of the ups and downs as well as the conveniences and inconveniences they experienced during the course of their relationships. But personally, I'd rather learn from other peoples' mistakes. Unfortunately, when it comes to dealing with matters of the heart, it seems more impacting and beneficial for others to experience pain and how to overcome failed relationships the old fashion way, through time and self perseverance.

The purpose of this material is not to dictate how a woman should think, behave or even act but to be cognizant of what it is she wants out of a relationship in conjunction with what a man looks for in a relationship.

A woman should not have to change or conform to what a man wants. She merely needs to find out what it is she wants, needs and what behaviors she is willing to tolerate during the course of her relationship. I've used actual accounts of not only my own experiences but the experiences of others to compile the information you're about to read. I want you to be informed as well as entertained. Most of all, I want this reading, as you indulge it, to be thought provoking while simultaneously giving you a sense of self awareness. Some of the scenarios may have you nostalgic or even remind you of someone who has gone through or is currently going through similar circumstances.

Let's face it, relationships, whether you're together or apart (physically) is like a full time job. Very rarely do we find that proverbial "*Soul mate.*" Please, do not misconstrue what I'm saying with it being nearly impossible to find a soul mate or someone you feel is compatible. I'm simply saying ladies should be practical based on what it is you're looking for in a relationship.

The concept of a lady acting like a lady but thinking like a man isn't very popular among men. I have interviewed many of my male colleagues, friends, and strangers alike who think that this is an antiquated perspective and is misleading to many women. Let me explain. I've heard this expression in the past and if I'm not mistaken, someone even wrote a book on this subject..! I can't imagine any man wanting his significant other to think like a man. It has often been said and proven by researchers and experts alike that our thoughts soon manifest into our actions. Do I need to elaborate? I think you know where I'm going with this. I make no attempts at trying to discredit anyone who chooses to shed light on the subject of relationships involving this concept. But honestly, there is a very good reason why there aren't two master chefs in the kitchen of a five star restaurant or two captains on an aircraft. (I will clarify later by what I mean.) What is it that we're (men) looking for? I, as many others feel that ladies should not only act like ladies but think like ladies as well.

A confident woman will have the capacity to know when a relationship is going awry. There are many women that chose to remain in a failing relationship. Based on my interviews, you will soon see why. One thing I've learned over the years, during my most intimate relationships, is that women have stronger intuitive abilities then men. They just fail to act upon them. Maybe even dismissing their feelings and justifying their man's behavior. Unfortunately, a lot of men need to conquer their desires (lower head) while women can fare better at controlling there emotions (upper head). I know what you're thinking, easier said then done, right? And perhaps you're right once you know what to look for. But after you've read the following, you'll soon realize where I'm going with this.

As mentioned previously, these stories are based on actual events but names and locations have been modified to protect the identities of those who willingly allowed me to use their stories. I thank the men and women who took time out of their busy schedules to accommodate me.

So I say to you, I hope you have as much fun reading my work as I had writing it. Read, learn and live life to the fullest...

Introduction

The many books that have been written on how a woman should act and think fail to encompass the fact that every woman enters a relationship for various reasons. With that being said, one man's ideologies of how she should think may apply to only a fraction of the female population.

The accounts you're about to have privy to will, in my opinion, change the way you enter any relationship. I feel this reading will help you make an informed decision as to whether or not the man you're with or even considering being with is right for you. In a short period of time (relative to what you're use to), you will be able to ascertain if this is the man you want to pursue, keep as a friend or drop like a bad habit. *Every woman has her reasons as to why she chooses to be involved in a relationship and should ask the question what's in it for me?* Does this sound selfish? What if I were to tell you we (men) do this all the time whether we realize it or not. It's only human to expect something when being involved with someone else. It's what the expectations are that makes the difference. This can range from wanting financial stability, companionship, having a father figure for your children or other desires of the heart that make you feel complete. Some relationships described, you yourself may have experienced or know someone who has.

I begin by revealing my own observations based on my previous relationships and the lessons that I've learned. It's really not that complicated. It's just a matter of knowing what it is you want, expect, and are willing to tolerate prior to even looking for a partner. I also want you, the reader to know that a man is not molded by what he does or how much he makes. His true character flaws will only be amplified with a surplus amount of money. In other words, if he were intolerable before he became successful, he will only be worse with added success. It is his values, morals and principles which are instilled in him, usually by his parents from an early age, that make him the individual he is now. So regardless of his salary, if he was an ass before he became successful he will still remain an ass even after reaching his goals. I say this because in recent books written it is insinuated that a man will be more secure with added finance resulting in him being a better man. A man will be more desirable in being in a fulfilling relationship if the woman he's with helps him to achieve his goals.

The task of finding out what you're willing to settle for proves often difficult when you are already in a relationship. This is why any woman contemplating pursuing a man should already have in mind why she wants to be in a relationship from the very beginning. This goes for both men and women. You see, it doesn't take a lot for you (ladies) to impress us. *A man can be infatuated and think he's in love, whereas a woman will be in love and think she's infatuated*. This is so because when a woman exits a tumultuous relationship, her emotions are guarded and is not ready to feel or except her emotions as being in love. For us, we fall in love with the exterior and mistaken infatuation for love. This usually happens in the beginning. You will see why in one of the scenarios presented. Let me explain. Men are superficial. It doesn't take a lot to impress us initially. It's keeping our attention that's the hard part. I make the analogy, *'A new relationship to a man is what a new video game is to a teenage boy."* Simple but profound if you really think about it. A man's attention needs to be kept initially and nurtured continuously if you have decided that you want this relationship to be long term. If the only thing a man has in common with his lady friend is good sex, that relationship will be short-lived. There has to be something else that will be captivating and entertaining as well as intellectually stimulating to both. The activity that a couple partakes in should be agreed to by both although both may not share the same enthusiasm. If there is any reluctance on his part, perhaps another activity should be chosen. After reading this, you will change the way you enter any relationship while avoiding the potential pitfalls and wasting valuable time.

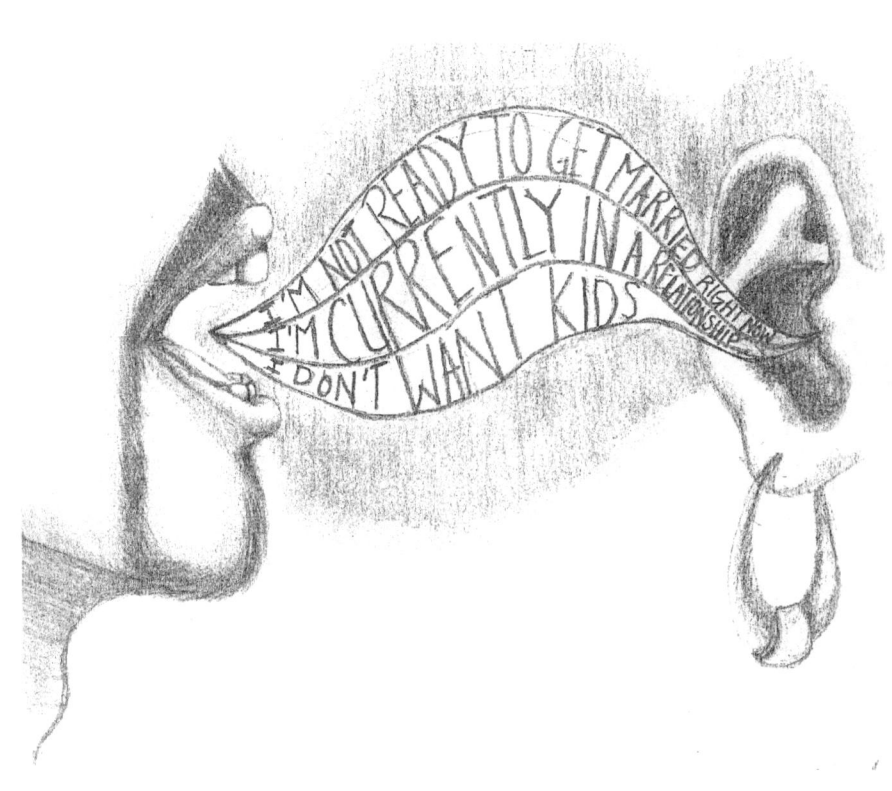

Chapter One

Are you Ready to Hear This?

Ladies, what if I was to tell you that much of your failed relationships could have been avoided. I know this may not be what you want to hear but it is the truth. Allow me to further explain why. I've heard women say time and time again, "I should have known better", or "he never seemed to care" or the classic, "I knew he wasn't right for me." I know what you're thinking right now, "what is your point?" Well let me reiterate on something I mentioned earlier. *A confident woman has the capacity to know when a relationship is in danger of going awry.* In other words you don't have to be told by your family members, mother, girlfriends or colleagues to know when it's simply not working out. You already have strong intuitive abilities to determine whether or not the man you're with is right for you. Despite this fact some women still remain in the relationship (sometimes even an abusive one) because they feel they can change the man they're with. Well I'm here to tell you, unless that man has exhibited to you in the past or present that he is willing to change, he's not going to. If you accepted or tolerated his unwanted or abusive behavior to begin with for any period of time, what makes you think he's going to change for you now?

While dating or seeking a potential mate a lot can go through a woman's mind in making the right decision. A man will quickly become very complacent in doing whatever he's accustomed to doing if you allowed this behavior in the beginning. In essence, if he told you from day one that he didn't want children or doesn't see marriage in the near future, why then would you think he would change his mind? With that being said, I present to you the first scenario.

The Scenario:

I should have known he didn't want to get married. Linda angrily thought this to herself as she left for work this morning. He always looked away from me whenever I asked him if he ever had plans on marrying me. We've been seeing each other for approximately three years now and every time I bought up the subject he looked away or would change the subject. It almost seemed as if he were sinking into his chair whenever I ask him. I remember him saying in the beginning that he had no interest in getting remarried because of his last divorce and often complained about how much the divorce set him back financially. Linda said to herself, "I'm going to call him and speak to him giving him an ultimatum or I'm walking."

That very same day, Linda called James during her lunch break to do just that. He seemed receptive to what I had to say and understanding as well Linda thought. Maybe he will give in and marry me after all, she thought to herself. The very next morning they met for breakfast at his place and Linda casually bought up the subject of marriage as she did on numerous occasions asking James if he made a decision. It was his usual routine every time Linda brought up the subject of marriage. James hesitated, looked away and gave Linda a non definitive answer, "honey how many times do I have to tell you, I can't afford to get married right now?" He further elaborated, "but I promise you once my finances are straight we can discuss *your dreams* of getting married then. You know I just finalized my divorce", James would politely explain. But for some reason, Linda no longer accepted a lack of money as being a legitimate excuse. Linda quickly explained, "Honey, if its money you're worried about, I can pay for the wedding and all you have to do is show up." (Big Mistake...See note at bottom of page). For this, James had no answer, so by James remaining silent, Linda started to make arrangements the following week for an elaborate wedding. The wedding was scheduled in the month of May for the following year and all of her friends and family were to attend. Linda was so excited that she even invited James' daughters who were products of his previous marriage. James' daughters did not agree with there relationship cause they often considered Linda much too old for their father. While James being 32 Linda was a stunningly attractive woman at 48 years of age and James daughters often referred to her as a cougar. Linda with two sons of her own to raise, was often the subject of controversy in James' household.

You see, Linda all ready had one failed marriage and unbeknownst to her, she was on her way to being divorced for a second time and didn't even know it. Linda seemingly was everything a man would want in a woman. She was a successful entrepreneur, attractive and very intelligent. She was also very assertive and well accustomed to getting what she wants. James himself was a foreman for a large construction company located in Manhattan, N.Y.. Needless to say, Linda spent nearly $80,000 on a wedding whereas the groom himself nor did any of his family members care to show up. Not only was Linda humiliated and trust that humiliation was the least of her worries. Linda would be in debt up to her neck for years to come and not to mention single once again.

> **Note:** I actually attended this wedding. I've read about the runaway bride, but the runaway groom..., now here's an interesting twist... Ladies, I know I shouldn't have to tell you this but whenever you have to bribe your man in to marrying you, something

is terribly wrong. I suggest ending the relationship during its infancy stages if marriage is important to you and he doesn't express any intentions on marrying at all.

The Lesson:

Linda knew that James had cold feet when it came to the subject of marriage. She knew of this at the very beginning of their relationship. Every time she mentioned marriage James would look away while he seemed to shrink in his chair and change the subject. His body language said it all. Even his responses indicated his distaste for being remarried. If you've noticed I purposely italicized his words, *"your dreams."* Simply put Linda's dreams of getting married were never his dreams and he referred to it as such.

When a man cares about you he will also care about what is important to you. Your dreams will become his or he will help you to achieve them if he plans on staying in a relationship with you. He will be interested in what you have to say and be attentive if the subject being discussed involves your future with him. Even if he is not interested in the subject being discussed, a man will still be attentive if he really loves you and cares about how you feel.

Linda, if a little bit more observant, would've picked up on his evasive gestures and attempts at changing the subject. After three years of observing this and his body language or attitude hasn't changed, guess what ladies, he's not going to change. I have to say, a man will be willing to change for the woman he is in love with. He will change financially, emotionally, and spiritually if he feels this is what you truly desire. ***Why, because love inspires people to do the things they normally wouldn't do.*** In this case she only saw what she wanted the outcome to be, and that was to be married once again. Linda made the mistake of discussing something so important to her over the phone. The subject of getting married or any topic of equal importance should never be discussed over the phone. I often advise others to refrain from discussing important matters of relationships over the phone. You want to observe his body language and see if his level of comfort contradicts his tone or words. This sounds like common sense, I know, but many women fall into this situation because of their strong desire to become married and being able to say, "this man belongs to me now." When in reality this is not what he wants at all. Not to mention James had this mind set from the beginning of their relationship so why would Linda expect him to change three years later? James has grown complacent over the three years they've been together. While Linda may have mentioned the subject of marriage a time or two in the past, she never got the response she was looking for. She also may have become very complacent in their relationship and didn't think that it would be an issue later on.

If you express to your significant other that you would like to eventually get married and ask "What are your feelings on getting married?" Check out his body language and listen to his response (more on body language in chapter 7). If he squares off his shoulders and crosses his arms, he has taken a defensive posture. He may also move backwards and away from you in his chair indicating that the subject being discussed is making him feel uncomfortable. People have a tendency to move away from the source causing them discomfort. During the course of a conversation, when a person pulls back and moves away from the source of discomfort, he/she is in disagreement with whatever the subject is being presented. These gestures indicated that the subject matter being presented to him is making him feel uneasy. Or if he constantly changes the subject when you bring it up, he simply doesn't want to discuss it and may have other plans for you.

Many women fail to realize that so much can be interpreted just by a man's body language alone. You just have to learn how to read them.

I've been asked to interview and sometimes even interrogate certain individuals for many years now in my line of work. I have the ability to determine if someone is uncomfortable or open to any suggestions or ideas I may present to them. There definitely is a pattern of behavior involved with truthfulness as well as deceit. If you know what to look for, it's like reading a book. There are plenty of books written on the subject of body language and non verbal communication. Learning how to discover when he is uncomfortable or up to something will save you a lot of heartache in the future. There are some exceptions however. For example, I wouldn't advise bringing up the subject of marriage or children on the first or second date unless he brings it up. Bringing up marriage or having children may, especially during the first couple of dates discourage him from continuing the relationship if that's the furthest thing from his mind.

So in a nutshell, it's good to let a man know your intentions and what you expect out of a relationship but if he's not responding accordingly, it may be time to throw in the towel. Take time to get to know each other better before bringing these two subjects up. Honesty is always the best policy but sometimes too much honesty during the beginning can cause a relationship to deteriorate. I know of a police officer who was dating a medical secretary. Everything seemed to be going very well until three weeks into their relationship she told him, "I want to be married and pregnant with my first child by the end of the year." Now at the time, marriage was the furthest thing from his mind and although he wanted children, he felt he wasn't ready to be a father just yet. Even if you felt it was meant to be, you may scare him away if you bring this subject matter up too soon. I know of another young man that recently started dating a restaurant manager. He couldn't stop talking about her for several weeks. He really considered getting serious with her until she mentioned that she wanted to get married and have kids. You see it's not that men don't want the responsibility of being a father or even getting married. Just give him a chance to develop feelings strong enough to want this just as bad as you do. If at the right and opportune time, the subject does happen to emerge, let him know how important this is to you.

Needless to say, his whole perspective changed and decided she was rushing into things. He decided that it would be best to remain friends. The funny thing is, he eventually wanted to get married, just not within the time parameter she wanted. Shame on you if your interests and what's important to you doesn't seem relevant to him and you've decidedly chose to ignore the signs. After all, body language is a great communicator!

A WOMAN SHOULD NOT HAVE TO CHANGE OR CONFORM TO WHAT A MAN WANTS. SHE MERELY NEEDS TO FIND OUT WHAT IT IS SHE WANTS, NEEDS AND BEHAVIORS SHE'S WILLING TO TOLERATE DURING THE COURSE OF THEIR RELATIONSHIP.

Chapter Two

What Exactly is It that You're Looking For?

Every woman has her own reason or reasons as to why she enters into a relationship. I've heard reasons range from financial security, stability and companionship. Commitment, security, family perceptions, children, and marriage are all legitimate concerns a woman may have prior to entering any relationship. Acts of love will often be reciprocated by a man when he feels you know what you want and aren't reluctant to show it. Each relationship you enter or depart should be a learning experience thus making you a more informed woman. A woman that knows what she wants and doesn't want will help to eliminate time being wasted.

It has often been said that a woman can determine within minutes as to whether or not she will become physically intimate with a man she has just met. So if you can determine something as deep and intimate as to whether or not you are going to sleep with someone, why not use that same ability and intuition to determine whether or not he may be right for you? Off course you won't be able to ascertain this right away but with good observation and listening skills, you will be able to do so within a relatively short period of time.

I would like to elaborate on a key point mentioned earlier. I stated that there is a very good reason why there aren't two master chefs in the kitchen of a five star restaurant or two captains on an aircraft. While in my early twenties I dated a nurse who would not hesitate for one moment to inform me of how independent she was and tell me how she didn't need a man to fulfill her needs. I often found this amusing because at the first sign of trouble I would be the one she would call for assistance. I would wonder, if she didn't need a man to fulfill her needs why be in a relationship at all?

During her interactions with her father, I noticed that he would cater to her whenever she needed anything. Her father would cook for her, pack her lunch before she left for work, do her laundry, wash her car etc. Alas, being young and immature, I blamed her father for her pampered ways. However, the more I analyzed the situation the more I realized that she didn't want a boyfriend, she wanted a father figure. She wanted me to cook, clean, and be at her beck and call as well as her lover all in the same ball of wax. I eventually sat her down and explained to her that I didn't think she was ready for a relationship and further explained that she wanted me to be just like her father. I couldn't compete with that so we decided to remain friends.

Not too long after I met Samantha. She was a kindergarten teacher and would do the opposite of whatever I suggested. For example, if she needed the oil changed on her car, I would suggest a nearby service station that I used and felt was reputable. She would in turn go to another station that would not only cost more but was at twice the distance. While vacationing together, I suggested taking the elevator because of the luggage we had in tow. I did so because our luggage was bursting at the seams. She ended up taking the escalator and nearly lost her luggage as a result.

Samantha didn't feel comfortable listening to what any man had to say or suggest if she didn't think of it on her own. She wanted to show her independence at any cost. In our conversations, I tactfully pointed this out to her. I asked if she lacked confidence in my judgment. She responded, "No." I presented my argument by giving examples and she simply felt she didn't need to listen to any man.

Needless to say, this relationship didn't last very long. A woman should know prior to any relationship what it is she's looking for. A woman that respects her man will allow him to make decisions that will be beneficial to you both. If she doesn't at least warrant him that, a man may feel unappreciated. Allow a man to make sound decisions and watch his increased level of confidence enhance the relationship. It is fine for a woman to succumb to her boyfriend's or husband's suggestions providing they're logical as well as reasonable. As long as you feel that trust, loyalty and honesty is reciprocated, given your significant other the benefit of the doubt will surely strengthen the relationship.

My interview with Jill...

During my research I interviewed Jill who is a marketing director from Delaware. She has been married twice. Jill explained that she recently moved into her boyfriend's house after approximately one year of seeing each other. Unbeknownst to her his dog, golf and Harley bike preoccupied most of his time. Surprisingly enough, it wasn't the lack of time being spent with her that was the chief complaint. It was his inability to get out of his miserable job he constantly complained about. His procrastination and her loosing respect for a man unwilling to make a change was causing their relationship to deteriorate. I asked her if she ever communicated her feelings to him.

Jill explained that she did so on numerous occasions but not one resume was ever submitted to seek new employment. Nor had he made any efforts to make a change. I asked Jill, "What if anything could he do to convince you to stay with him?" Jill responded, "If he started posting his resume in an attempt to find new employment then I would have admiration and respect for him. However, all I hear him do is complain and he doesn't do anything to improve his situation."

I then asked Jill, "What was it that drew you to him in the first place?" Jill replied, "The passion, the dinners, the courtship and being loved was an exciting novelty I cherished in the beginning. Intellectual stimulation is also very important. I admired his passion for the things he likes. (Golf, motorcycles etc) I feel that on his days off something productive should come out of it." Jill further explained that her boyfriend grew complacent. He fell into a routine that no longer stimulated their relationship. Jill admits that although she feels he is in love with her, she is not in love with him. She loves him and cares for him but is not in love. (See chapter #10 for the difference) Jill confessed that her breaking up with him is the inevitable. Although sexually compatible, this would not be enough to keep them together. Majority of the time men don't continue to do the same things they did during the infancy of the relationship. Being sexually compatible may keep you together for a period of time but it won't be the adhesive that will keep you together for very long.

In the beginning, we act on our instincts when we're attracted to someone. That instinct may even lead to a one night stand. A woman will know this way before a man even has a clue as to what your intentions really are.

Just as men act on instinct so do woman at times. Statistically speaking a woman wants it just as bad as men do. She just has better control over her desires and more options. Interestingly enough, while a man can be considered physically unattractive, his options will be limited while a woman; no matter how unattractive she may be or feel, her choices will be plentiful. No matter how unattractive you may feel or think you are, someone will think just the opposite and see you as being beautiful just the way you are. Whereas a man can be physically unattractive and more than likely find it difficult at finding the woman of his dreams or desirable to him.

On another note, a woman should try not to be too inquisitive about his finances in the very beginning of the relationship. This is a sure way to discourage a man from considering a long term relationship with you. Again, there are exceptions to the rule. If he enjoys bragging about how much he makes and boasts about his material possessions then it is open for discussion.

Let's say you have been dating for a while, several months now and it's getting serious. He decides to take you on a cruise. "Great!" you think. Then he ends up asking you for half the cruise ticket money. Would this upset you or make you reconsider? What if your date decided it would be better if you both were to meet at the theater as opposed to him picking you up? What would you think? What if he was running late and asked you to cook dinner? Would this be out of the question?

I ask these questions because as odd as it may seem, I've met women that said they wouldn't appreciate a man asking them to pay in the beginning and would rather be picked up than met. Some women are too busy or tired to cook when returning home from work. They wouldn't give a man they dated a time or two another date if he asked her to chip in. What about a man declining a dinner date due to babysitting issues or overtime at work? Would this be enough for you to lose interest?

Questions such as these will help you determine what it is you're really looking for in a man. The point I'm driving at is that a woman can be more selective about who she chooses to be with based on the conversations she has with a potential mate. Before entering any relationship, you should be able to decide what it is you want out of that relationship prior to getting serious. What criteria have you established while considering being with someone? If it is financial security you want, why would you date a pizza delivery guy? If it's a guy you want that takes pride in his health and you yourself enjoy working out, would you date an overweight guy who smokes like a chimney? Absolutely not! I see time and time again women who date guys that they are totally incompatible with. Then they complain about the guy being lazy, out of shape, unemployed or still sleeping on his mother's couch. But yet and still, they stay with him until either a) they find someone better or b) eventually get tired of him and leave.

If you knew from the beginning that the guy that's interested in you isn't your type, why waste your time as well as his? Consider this scenario:

The Scenario:

"Jimmy can be so immature at times", Carmella explained to her mother as she did her laundry one Sunday afternoon. Carmella went on as she did every Sunday afternoon, while exchanging family gossip about her boyfriend. She explained that her boyfriend loved going to clubs and never wanted to do anything she enjoyed doing. "I purchased Broadway tickets to the play *"Microphone Speaks"* for next Saturday but he just ignores me when I tell him about it. I really don't know what to do or how to get him interested in the things I like to do." Carmella's mother explained, "well honey you dated on and off for nearly two years now and if he hasn't changed by now he never will."

Carmella always wanted a man who enjoyed the same things she did but Jimmy seemed to be the complete opposite. She enjoyed plays, while Jimmy frequented clubs. She liked to take leisurely strolls at the beach or in the park while Jimmy would rather stay home and play video games. On some occasions, Jimmy would oblige Carmella and accompany her to the beach, park and sometimes a play. Reluctantly, Jimmy would attend but showed little interest. The only thing they seemed to have in common was good sex and even that began to decline. Carmella was an attractive woman in her late 30s who often declined Jimmy's advances when she was angry at him. This happened quite often. Jimmy would conform to whatever Carmella wanted to do. Unbeknownst to Carmella, every time she would use sex as a weapon, (see note) he would simply pay a visit to his ex-girlfriend who would be more than happy to oblige him. She often complained to her mother who recited an old proverb in response to Carmella's disappointment, *"You can lead a horse to water but you can't make him drink it."* In other words, you cannot make someone become interested in something he is not. You can introduce him to new things but if he's not interested or doesn't make an attempt to be open minded to what it is you have to offer, it is simply not going to work.

> (Note: Using sex as a weapon. I only have one thing to say ladies… **DON'T DO IT!** This is a very ineffective method at trying to get him to conform to what you want. It ultimately drives him to find it elsewhere. I experienced this while in my early twenties and would take a trip to my ex's place. Although majority of the time sexual maturity does come with age and experience, a man who lacks control over his desires will resort to the quick fix.

The Lesson:

You see Carmella wanted a man for companionship. There is absolutely nothing wrong with that. She should have conveyed her interests to him in the beginning of their relationship. Carmella wanted someone who would accompany her to plays, strolls on the beach and so forth. Prior to entering this relationship, Carmella didn't take the time out to communicate exactly what it is she was looking for in the relationship. Carmella saw an attractive man, who took care of himself and was an aspiring photographer but failed to realize she had little if anything in common with him.

Carmella never really took the time out to ask herself, "What exactly is it that I'm looking for in a man?" Once determined, Carmella should've found out whether or not her new boyfriend shared common interests. Now I'm not saying that she shouldn't have given Jimmy a chance. What I am saying is she could have considered him as a friend and expressed to him that they lack same interests. She settled for his ways and was very unhappy as a result.

The moral of the story is, ***know what it is you want and expect out of a man before you pursue a relationship with him***. In addition, find out what it is you are willing to accept or do without while being in a relationship. It is ok to make sacrifices but not when it compromises your own happiness. All relationships consist of sacrifices. If he is not willing to join you in the things you enjoy doing, find something that you both can partake in and have fun together. Without him pouting or sulking like a little child. We tend to do that at times when we don't get our way. In addition, using sex as a weapon to get what you want is a **BIG** mistake. I know what you're thinking. What gives me the right to tell a woman how and when to have sex and under what circumstances? I'm here to tell you ladies, if you want to encourage your man to cheat, use sex as a weapon. If you have to resort to such extreme measures in order for your significant other to hang out with you, you are with the wrong guy. I know I've been told time and time again that a woman's sexual desires are attached to their emotions. Ladies, know what you are getting into before you become deeply involved.

Some time ago I asked a female colleague of mine, "Why do women tend to fall in love so easily?" She inquired, "Well, did you sleep with her?" I responded quizzically, "Yes I did sleep with her." She went on to explain that when a woman gives her body to a man, she feels a sense of entitlement. Or the man she give herself to should be obligated to her. Men do not feel this way. Men do not usually get emotional when it comes to sex. Unless however, he is in love with the woman he is making love to. Passion and a connection will be felt by both the man and the woman if both are in love. If a man is not in love he will simply go through the motions and when he's done you will know that the relationship you are involved in lacks the spark, passion or connection you are looking for.

Years ago I remember telling a woman that I wasn't looking for a relationship. She agreed and said neither was she. After only a couple of months, she became very possessive and told me she loved me. I never responded and this would upset her as she would ask, "Why don't you ever tell me I love you back?" I would simply ask, "Why would you want me to lie?" If a man is telling you that he is not ready for children, marriage or anything serious, take what he is telling you seriously. Especially if this is what you desire.

More often than not, the method of withholding sex from your man is sure to lead to him being unfaithful. In his mind, this only gives a man who already has wandering eyes more justification to cheat. So in a nutshell, know what it is you want out of a relationship before entering one. Make it clear to him so that there will be no misunderstanding or confusion as to what it is you are looking for.

A CONFIDENT WOMAN WILL HAVE THE CAPACITY TO KNOW WHEN A RELATIONSHIP IS GOING AWRY.

Chapter 3

Be Honest with yourself

Be honest with yourself. This is one of the most difficult things a woman could do when she is in a relationship. I say this because I often hear of women complaining about their boyfriends, fiancés and husbands alike and still claim that they are happy. Is it a façade that you want or feel you need to maintain? Are family members putting pressure on you to get marriage and have kids? Perhaps it's because he provides you with financial security, emotional support or makes for a great companion. Or maybe you feel that you may have a future with this man because of his ambitions. I often find that a career oriented woman will not be happy placing her future on hold in order to accommodate her man. What happens once he has accomplished whatever it is he is trying to do? What if he decides he no longer needs you? The time you had vested in a relationship would've been wasted.

Unless you are married, why would you place everything you ever dreamed of on hold for someone you may or may not even be with very long? Why can't you accomplish your goals together? This to me seems like a no-brainer when a woman thinks she has met the man of her dreams than turns around and is asked to postpone her own dreams. How would you react if this was asked of you?

If a man has your best interest at heart, he will devise a plan in which you both can accomplish your goals while pursuing future endeavors. A man will rarely ever say, "Honey, why don't you finish school while I stay home and watch the kids." Therefore, why would you concede to something of the sort? If you both are goal driven, you now have a common goal and will help each other achieve it. Compromise and sacrifice must take place and your trials and tribulations will come to past. This often strengthens a relationship when a couple endures their struggles together.

I believe that the good Lord wants all of his children to be happy. That is why a good woman desirous of a successful relationship needs to learn how to **L**isten, **O**bserve, **R**eevaluate and **D**ecide whether or not she should remain in her current relationship. Allow me to break it down in further detail.

LISTEN

Listening is easier said then done. To hear and to listen are two different things. Anyone can hear someone, something or anything which produces sound. It takes attentiveness to be able to listen. Not everyone is capable of interpreting what it is they are hearing. This is because people want what they are hearing to work to their advantage. Does the term *selective hearing* sound familiar? Are you still unclear? What if I were to tell you that when interested in someone, it would be advantageous for you, the listener, to take in what the mother, sister, female family members or friends have to say. I have often heard women say, his sister told me or his mother warned me, but I wasn't paying them any mind or didn't take what they were saying seriously.

You see a potential boyfriend's or husband's family can be a wealth of information if you know how to listen. Families often, without realizing it, reveal a lot about a man's past. Especially the mother if you learn to establish a good rapport with her. Have her join you for a luncheon and just sit back and listen to what she has to say. Go shopping or to the mall with his sister while listening to her complain about her brother's good and bad habits. (Catch her on the day her brother pissed her off) She will be more than happy to rat him out or make fun of his past relationships. Learning how to listen will give you a relatively good idea as to what you are dealing with or maybe even explain some of his behaviors. Remember ladies, effective communication often stems from people who are good listeners.

OBSERVE

This one goes along with being a good listener but I felt further clarification was in order. If after listening to his family and you still decide he has potential, proceed on to becoming a good observer/spectator. Listening and being a good observer can be done simultaneously. This is self explanatory for the most part. Simply observe his interactions with friends, family and colleagues at various functions, especially female co-workers. If he invites you to his office Christmas party you should attend. When he invites you to his father's BBQ you should attend. Any function that will allow him to be comfortable being himself while in his own element will often show a man's true character.

See if he acts indifferent towards you when around female co-workers. Does he seem nervous, outgoing, or withdrawn? Does he behave differently when he is around others? Learning to be a good observer of his behaviors at functions will often be a good indicator as to what kind of man he really is and what lies ahead for you.

REEVALUATE / RECONSIDER

Now its time to reevaluate what it is your relationship is all about. Does he make you happy? Is he respectful and considerate of your needs? Most importantly, is this someone you can see yourself being with for the duration? Contemplate what it is you like about him and what behaviors you find unacceptable or simply annoying. Maybe even write a pros and cons or a likes and dislikes list. Ask yourself, and again be honest while asking, "What's keeping me with this guy, or better yet, what's preventing me from leaving him? If the list you create results in the cons outweighing the pros, you may have to make a decision as to why you are still with him. Does he have a great sense of humor, is he intellectually stimulating? Or is it that you are both sexually compatible? Maybe he's great with the kids. Reconsider all of your options before it's too late.

DECIDE

This is often difficult to do especially if you decide to end it. This goes for the man as well. No one wants to hurt someone they have been intimate with both emotionally and physically. Usually unless a woman is scorned by infidelity or the equivalent does she then seek to end a relationship without too much collateral damage. But maybe I'm being a bit pessimistic here. What if you decide to stay? Then ultimately, you have decided that the time vested in this relationship is worth it. The little things he does that seem to annoy you are somewhat tolerable and can be overlooked. Congratulations, you have made a decision to be in a productive relationship!

Chapter 4

The Writing is On the Wall

Many women have confided in me with concern and asked advice as to why their man is behaving a certain way or doing the things he is doing. Majority of the time we do the things we do or act in certain ways based on your reactions. For example, a very good friend of mine once told me that her fiancé would leave dirty dishes in the sink, leave clothes on the floor after he came from work and wouldn't shower before he came to bed at night. She even had to buy this guy a toothbrush! Although his lack of hygiene bothered her, she never took the time out to tell him that it did. They dated for ten months before they decided to live together.

Do you think his behavior changed or hygiene improved once they moved in together? Off course not! So his lack of cleanliness that annoyed her prior to living with him only became worse. Needless to say, I had to ask her, "Why would you expect him to change if this is something he was accustomed to doing?" She just looked at me quizzically and said, "I thought I could change him." Maybe if she would have expressed her concerns to him prior to moving in, he might've have changed for the better. Needless to say, they had a horrible breakup.

Let me give you this analogy. Would you go to a car dealership and buy a car without sitting in it or even test driving it? I don't think most people would purchase a vehicle without test driving it. You would walk around the car, admiring its details while asking numerous questions. If still interested, then perhaps, maybe a test drive would be in order. You may still request additional information before finalizing your decision. This is how you should be with a potential mate. Be more analytical while becoming more informed and don't rush into things. If you just came out of a relationship let him know. That way he will know why you may feel apprehensive about certain things.

Let me share this story with you regarding an old friend who had her life turned upside down. She said to me after her failed attempt at being married and tens of thousands of dollars in debt, "*The writing was on the wall.*" To this day, she is still recovering.

The Scenario:

Everyone tried to tell me but I just would not listen. Stacy angrily thought to herself as she took the LIRR home from Brooklyn that night.

Stacy married a man named Craig who was from the West Indies and was extremely attracted to him. He was everything she ever wanted in a man, she would often say to her girlfriends. Craig was handsome, intelligent, and had a decent job working as a plumber. In addition, Craig knew how to show Stacy the kind of chivalry she has never known. He knew that Stacy loved when he opened doors for her, helped her put on her coat before going out, and pulling out the chair while being seated at her favorite restaurant. This was short lived after several dates. Although he contributed to the household expenses it never seemed enough. Craig and Stacy decided to get married after only eleven months. Prior to their marriage, he often would pressure Stacy to have a civil wedding so that they could save money. Unbeknownst to her, he was living a lie. You see Craig was living illegally in the United States and would often tell Stacy that he wanted to marry her within months of their relationship because of the strong love he felt for her. He wanted to attain status as a U.S. resident. Craig was also very quick to ask her for money. Stacy didn't seem to mind, making a six figure salary while working as a civil rights attorney for a prestigious law firm. With Stacy's lucrative career money never seemed to be an issue.

Craig obliged her in whatever it was she wanted to do as long as she paid. When hanging out with the girls, she would often be accused of being naïve and blind. You see, looking in from the outside, Stacy's girlfriends noticed that he never paid for anything, nor did he ever invite her out and seemed very uncomfortable whenever her friends were around. It was always Stacy that would take the initiative and make the dinner reservations. In addition, he spent a lot of time at home rather then at work.

Craig often complained about his car breaking down which prevented him from working. Stacy went to a dealership and purchased him a car. Then came the excuses of him being too sick to work so he would end up staying home. It came to a point, whereas the only thing Stacy and Craig had was their marriage and a small condo located in the suburbs.

Being that Stacy wasn't really close to her mother, she didn't confide in her as much. However, her father sure had a lot to say and would often tell his daughter, "baby, this guy is a loser, get rid of him before its too late." While Craig sat at home, the bills began to accumulate. Bills that Craig claimed to have paid now had debt collectors calling their home at various times of the day. Their car was in jeopardy of being repossessed and the condo was in total disarray. Stacy rushed into marriage with a man she hardly knew anything about. Craig offered her money one time when she showed reluctance in marrying him. She took this as a joke and dismissed it as such. She never knew Craig's family and when she inquired, Craig would simply say, "They don't live in the states but you will soon meet them." Nonetheless, Stacy still married Craig without meeting his family.

Being an educated and well informed woman that she considered herself to be, 'I shouldn't be in this situation', she thought to herself. Although the signs were there, and family and friends alike attempted to warn her, she thought of them as being envious. Dad was just being over protective.

Long story short, she married a guy she barely knew and suffered the consequences. In retrospect, had she paid attention, and perhaps heeded some of the warnings given to her, she would have realized that this relationship was only benefiting Craig. He had everything to gain and nothing to lose. Unfortunately the same couldn't be said of Stacy.

Stacy was married and divorced within eighteen months. The debt she incurred will take several years to overcome not to mention the disappointment of being in a failed marriage. She has learned a valuable lesson and realizes now that she shouldn't have rushed into marriage with a man she barely knew anything about.

Adrian Weber

Miss C's Dilemma

I recently had the opportunity of interviewing a very energetic and spirited woman who resides in Queens, New York. As an attractive and successful woman, after the interview, I couldn't help but to wonder why she would limit herself so. She's an educator and a mother of two. I refer to her during my interview as Miss C. My line of questioning although direct didn't make her feel uncomfortable but was indeed thought provoking. I started by informing her of my intentions to reveal in my work that women, as mentioned previously have stronger intuitive abilities then men but fail to act upon them for various reasons. I just couldn't help but to wonder why it is they allow themselves to continue, long after seeing the signs, to be in a tumultuous relationship.

I basically set this up as a Q & A session. Not being surprised, but more so intrigued by her answers I found them to be somewhat typical. It also made me wonder how an educated and well rounded woman such as herself didn't end the relationship to nowhere from the very beginning. Here is what I found out.

Interview with Miss C.

AW: Good evening Miss C. I would first like to thank you for allowing me the privilege of being able to interview you.

Miss C: It's my pleasure, thank you for the privilege.

AW: I would first like to begin by asking you, can you recall a past relationship whereas you knew it felt wrong but continued to be in it anyway?

Miss C: Yes, not too long ago I was involved with a man I felt extremely compatible with. I thought he felt the same until after we became married.

AW: Well, what happened? How long after you guys met did you get married?

Miss C.   Well things were a bit complicated in the beginning. I wanted everything, his time, financial security, companionship, and a family. I often complained about him not spending enough time with me often driving him out of the house. I complained a lot and it was all about me and I was being selfish.

AW: I think these wants were reasonable requests. You mentioned that things were complicated. Can you elaborate?

Miss C.   Well, when I first met him, he was involved with a woman he had two kids in common with. **He was**

**with her for ten years. He then left her after only
two weeks of meeting me.**

AW: I have to ask you this. If he was willing to leave the
mother of his children after ten years only after being
with you for two weeks, didn't this concern you? I
mean, what's to stop him from doing this to you?

Miss C: You're right and eventually he did just that but I was
blindsided. I didn't want to think that he would. It's
not that he wasn't capable, but I didn't think that he
would do this to me! He fell out of love with her and
no longer wanted to be with her because of her abusive
and manipulative ways. She didn't really love him like
I did. He only stayed with her because of the children
they had in common.

AW: You mentioned that you were blindsided, how so?

Miss C.   **He showered me with gifts, lavish dinners and great
vacations.** He was also very good with my kids. I
liked that he wasn't selfish or abusive. He wined and
dined me, gave me nice gifts, and I loved the way he
interacted with my kids. Not to mention, we had a
lot in common. You see, I came out of a very abusive
relationship while being with my children's father and
so did he.

AW: You said he also came out of an abusive relationship.
Can you elaborate?

Miss C: Yes, his children's mother would verbally abuse him and constantly use his kids as a weapon against him if she didn't have her way.

AW: So what happened, you mentioned you guys got married?

Miss C.   Yes, we did in a short period of time. I didn't want to lose him because I wanted that family structure. He proposed to me after only three weeks and we were married in four months. Although we didn't date very long before getting married, I knew him for some time before we started dating.

AW: Proposal in three weeks, marriage in four months? Didn't you think that was too soon?

Miss C: At the time, no. But retrospectively speaking, if I could turn back the hands of time, I would've taken my time and got to know him a little better.

AW: Why would you have taken your time, what happened?

Miss C.   *(Laughs...)* what happened? Hah, you mean what didn't happen….!
             Prior to getting married, **he would always hide me from his family**. I thought this was strange and would often get upset about it. But then he would explain that his ex was so vindictive that if she were to find out about our marriage, she wouldn't allow him to see

his kids. So I *partially* accepted this explanation until I met his grandmother.

AW: What happened?

Miss C: Well, while running some errands, I ran into his grandmother. She wanted to know why I wouldn't bring the kids over to see her. Without volunteering too much info, I told her, "I'm just trying to keep the peace." "His ex is very spiteful and will prevent him from seeing the kids." During the course of our conversation, she inadvertently revealed to me that he has two other kids from a previous relationship. My jaw dropped and I couldn't believe how stupid and naïve I was to think that he was behaving this way because of his ex.

AW: So why did you think he was behaving this way?

Miss C: Come on, you know... He hid me from his family because he knew eventually they would expose him for the liar that he really was. I mean, I should've known something was up. He would keep me from his family. He fooled me and my entire family..! On top of that, the money dried up.

AW: How so?

Miss C: **He no longer took me to dinner, or bought me expensive gifts. I would leave for work in the morning only to return and see him on the couch in the same position I left him in.** I then found out that he was still seeing his ex. That pretty much was the proverbial straw that broke the camel's back.

AW: I have to ask you what it was beside the gifts, dinners and trips, that ultimately led you into marrying this guy? Clearly, you have your own home, car and seem to be maintaining a comfortable lifestyle all on your own. Were you perhaps on the rebound?

Miss C: Yes, I was. Besides spoiling me, he was great with my kids. When he would go shopping, he would shop for everyone. I loved the way he treated and respected my children. I also thought we had a lot in common since we both were and came out of abusive relationships. He treated me the total opposite of how my ex treated me. He gave me a lot of attention too. The funny thing about it was, in the beginning, I really wasn't interested in him. But he was so persistent and I thought to myself, "I can get used to this." Being spoiled that is. He simply grew on me. Shortly before my marriage ended, I came to find out a lot about his past and present. He wasn't at all who he said he was and lied about his previous relationships, employment and just about everything. **I was angry at myself for rushing into things but I learned from this experience and matured from it as well.**

AW: If you could list the things that went wrong from the beginning of this relationship, what would they be?

Miss C: Well first off, he made sure to keep me away from his family. I mean I somewhat understood or accepted his justifications for not wanting me to interact with his family prior to marrying him because of his spiteful ex. After marriage, I figured the cat was outta the bag. No BBQs, weddings, or any family functions would he bring me to. For some reason, the money ran out shortly after we married. He would constantly lie about where his money was going. Then came the, "by chance encounter", with his grandmother. She revealed to me that he had two other children. Last but not least, I had to call it quits after I found out he was still with his ex.

AW: Now I have to ask you, if there is any advice you would give to the ladies out there in order to avoid a situation such as the one you just described, what would it be?

Miss C: #1 priority, take your time. Don't rush into things. Find out more about him and don't be afraid to ask him about the things you're curious about or things that concern you. I didn't ask enough questions. Perhaps I knew the answers and didn't want to hear them. I was initially pleased with what he had to offer. Meet his family… I'll say it again, unless you're in another country and the family is distant, meet his family before getting too serious. The one time I spoke to his grandmother, I learned about his other two kids.

AW: Well Miss C. I would like to thank you once again for sharing this with me and hope that your advice reaches enough women to help them make the right decisions.

The Lesson:

Now let's take a moment to analyze this interview if you will. Although Miss C had reasonable requests, she was willing to overlook and tolerate many of her husband's shortcomings. If you noticed, I have bolded some parts of her statements to indicate *"red flags."* She noticed the red flags but admits she was blindsided because of the lavish gifts she was given. If you also noticed, I italicized Miss C's term, *"partially accepted,"* when she described the circumstances of being hidden from his family. Her words indicated that her intuition was telling her something was up. Miss C felt that the man she was about to marry hid her for reasons other than his vindictive ex but her strong desire to become married rationalized his explanation.

Many men lie by omission and fail to reveal a lot about their past, present and future intentions. This could be for many reasons, not necessarily to hurt the woman that they are with but to spare their feelings in some instances or they may look for an opportune time to reveal certain things. I find that men withhold tidbits of information during the infancy of a relationship in fear of ruining a potential relationship. This is especially so when a man wants to be with you long term. Men do not generally withhold important information in order to have sex with you as many women would suspect but often look for the right time to tell you. Now this is not to say that revealing certain things will inhibit a man's chances of having sex with you because as I and many of my male friends and interviewees found out, women find it to be extremely attractive when a man is honest and direct with you from the very beginning. Women find a man that is honest from the beginning to be confident and unafraid of sharing his past with you.

I also find that many women, although disappointed in some of the revelations she is privy to will still be intimate with a man if she feels comfortable and doesn't feel compromised.

While in my early twenties, I would tell a woman I've recently met that I'm currently involved with someone. Despite this, she would still be interested in pursuing a relationship. When I asked why she was still interested, she would say she appreciated my honesty. Back to the lesson at hand, I will translate each bolded excerpt in detail.

1. **He was with her for ten years. He then left her after only two weeks of meeting me.**

If a man can so willingly and easily leave a woman he has been with for ten years for a woman he just met two weeks ago, he has loyalty issues. A man capable of doing this has no remorse, principles or morals if he can leave the mother of his children after only two weeks of meeting another woman. Now I'm not saying he should remain in an abusive relationship because of the children he has in common with her. However, he should communicate to her how he feels and what his intentions are while still being a father to his children.

2. **He showered me with gifts, lavish dinners and great vacations.**

Anytime a man feels the need to impress you with expensive gifts, and extravagant vacations he feels the need to overcompensate. He may have issues with insecurity or feelings of inadequacies that he may not want you to notice. He may not be able to spend as much time as you would want him to spend with you so he buys you gifts in order to distract you from what his real intentions are. Don't pay too much attention to what it is a man buys for you as did Miss C. She should have been more concerned with why he feels the need to buy her love and affection with expensive gifts.

I have heard women say that a romantic walk on the beach, park or even a card and some flowers is sufficient enough to let her know that you care about the relationship. It's the simple and thoughtful gestures that mean a lot. Now don't get me wrong, there's nothing wrong with receiving nice gifts but at the beginning of any relationship, a woman should be somewhat suspicious if this is all a man has to offer.

3. He would always hide me from his family.

Excuse me for saying this but in my opinion this is common sense. If a man attempts to hide you from his family, it is because he himself has something to hide. Now unless the man comes from an orphanage, has been adopted or his family members are deceased, there is absolutely no excuse why a man should have to hide you. Now it is true that there are women that can be vindictive and use the children in common as a weapon. Eventually after getting married, a woman should become familiar with some of the family. At minimum, the parents or siblings should be introduced prior to getting engaged if you decide to remain in the relationship.

4. He no longer took me out to dinner, or bought me expensive gifts.

Once a man stops buying you gifts and doing the things he did during his initial courtship it is time to reevaluate the relationship.

During the beginning, you met what I commonly like to refer to as his *representative.*

Let me explain. You see, we (men) want to impress you. So if we feel we can impress you with nice gifts, fancy dinners and luxurious vacations, that's what we'll do. We will read you and decide what makes you tick. We want to know through conversation what it is we need to do or get in order to impress you and keep you interested. A man can often determine this by the way you react to what it is you see while we are with you. For example, if a man takes you out and you comment on how beautiful a certain car is, he will know that nice cars impress you. So what do we do? No matter what kind of car we are driving, whether a late or old model car, we will get that car washed and the tires covered in armor all.

If we walk past a florist and notice you admiring an arrangement of yellow roses, we will eventually surprise you with them. Now if he continues to do this for the duration, he's being sincere in his gifts and intentions are to be with you long term. He will do this because he knows this is what pleases you and makes you happy.

A man will also do this and more in order to leave the impression upon you that he will do anything to please you. That is until he gets what he wants. This could be anything from sex to money, borrowing your car or maybe he needs a place to stay. If he is not consistent with the chivalry and gifts he exhibited at the beginning then that was merely his *representative.*

5. I was angry at myself for rushing into things.

Miss C has a valid point here. Whenever women rush into relationships, especially after just coming out of one, this shows desperation. You don't want to be the rebound girl. Entering any relationship after just getting out of one isn't conducive to you having a successful new relationship. This is because you have not given yourself time to heal or to figure out what caused your last relationship come to an end. I met a woman who, after a failed relationship, would take a break for two years before getting seriously involved with anyone again.

She wanted to be sure that her affairs were in order and that she was over the last guy before entering into another relationship. Once you have decided to end a relationship, try to take some time out to know what it is you're looking for. (see chapter #2) What do you expect out of the relationship and are you even ready to be in one? (see chapter #6) Miss C never gave herself a chance to heal and was on the rebound. She admits that she didn't want to be alone. This is the best time to give yourself a rest from any obligations or demands that come with being in a relationship. Well as with many other women, Miss C later realized that *the writing was on the wall*.

Chapter 5

Listen to His Mom (being a good listener)

I can't stress enough how important this concept really is. In the interest of not only wasting his time but more importantly yours as well, I suggest you highlight this chapter title for future reference. Mothers, as mentioned previously, are a wealth of information. They often reveal things (often warnings) about their sons, unintentionally, that if heeded, will save you a lot of time and energy. A family member revealed to me that her future mother-in-law often warned her about her own son. Her mother- in- law would sorrowfully say to her, "Du tuts mir leid" (German) literally translated as, "I feel sorry for you." I don't know about you but if my future mother-in-law told me that, I think I would run for the hills! Or at least find out more about why his own mother would make such a statement.

She later realized that the man she married was not only an alcoholic but had many other issues to contend with that resulted in them being divorced. She never really took the time out to ask why her mother-in-law often said this to her. Had she been a bit more inquisitive and asked her to elaborate further, she would've possibly avoided much strife and heartache.

I know of another whose mother-in-law pretty much spelled it out for her! Meaning she basically sat her down and told her that her son was very irresponsible and could not be depended on. He is not the most mature person and was warned to be careful of any financial decisions she made with him. In this case, she heeded the warning and ended up leaving him before it was too late. She did this only after becoming aware of her fiancé's plan to use her credit to buy a motorcycle and a new car.

Now don't get me wrong. I'm not saying that you shouldn't help your significant other. I'm merely suggesting that you make yourself aware of what his intentions are. Is he constantly leaning on you for financial support? I remember years ago, I was going through some difficult times. I asked my ex that I was living with at the time to get an additional credit card under my name so that I could strengthen my credit. Without any hesitation she said no. At the time, we were together for a few years and paying the household expenses together. I did not consider it to be an issue. It wasn't that I was financially irresponsible I simply was overwhelmed because of a pay cut I endured during my new career.

I just started my new job and was always employed. Unfortunately my father's business partner reneged on a business agreement that ultimately caused a financial crisis. I wasn't asking her to co-sign or pay any bills for me. I simply asked if she could get an additional card under my name that she would keep and use. I thought it was pretty inconsiderate of her not to warrant me that request but in retrospect, I see why she decided the way she did.

Sometimes we enter relationships where one maybe a little more financially stable than the other. However this imbalance should not deter you from pursuing a long lasting and possibly lucrative relationship. I say lucrative because when two people come together and combine resources, a lot can be accomplished. A relationship that may eventually lead to you both being happily married while being financially blessed. Many couples split due to disagreements on how money should be spent. You may see a fur coat you have been eyeing up for quite some time while he may see a late model car in the near future. I've heard of couples arguing while having plenty of money to accommodate all their needs but still disagreeing on what to spend it on. Here's an interesting statistic. Although it still can become an issue to some. There is much more to a relationship than money alone. He may be contributing in other ways; with his time, things he does around the house or you may like the way he interacts with your children. Or you may simply just enjoy being with him.

As with any rule or suggestion, there will always be exceptions. For example, there are some mothers out there whereas they don't believe in divorce or believe their sons can do no wrong. Several years ago I had a friend who left an abusive marriage. Her husband was physically, verbally and emotionally abusive to her. No matter how many times she confided in her mother-in-law about her son's behavior, she would always attempt to justify his abusive ways. Some mothers do not believe in divorce and will try to convince you to stay. Staying in an abusive relationship is not an option. If you have children they will be affected adversely. While growing up they will think that abusive relationships is typical and part of being in any relationship.

At this time I would like the reader to see from a woman's perspective what signs are given when a man has the potential to be abusive and how you can avoid being in an abusive relationship.

Recognizing the Signs...

(Physical, Verbal and Emotional Abuses)

Ladies, if he is abusive, the writing will definitely be on the wall. Think of the wall containing letters which make you feel horrible each time you dare to read them or even glance at it. This is what domestic violence is filled with, ugly letters that spells out the wrong ingredients in any relationship.

Having witnessed this ugly monster for over a decade and knowing women who have escaped abusive relationships; I recognize the signs when it comes to domestic violence and no woman should stay in an abusive relationship. If in the beginning of any relationship, a man gestures or hints at wanting to strike you during an argument or disagreement, he may have a propensity for being physically abusive. If this man hurls profanities at you or attempts to belittle and degrade you while having a heated discussion, he may have a tendency to be verbally abusive.

Many times it starts out with verbal abuse and progresses into physical abuse. Then there is emotional abuse where a man constantly criticizes you for anything and everything you do. This can range from the way you cook to the way the house is kept. He may put you down about your weight or appearance. A man that loves you will be honest with you if your weight concerns him but will be more compassionate in his delivery. For example, if he feels you may be overweight, he may suggest as a new year's resolution, getting a gym membership for the two of you and work out together. He may even take up some cooking classes so that you both may eat healthier. He will be encouraging and uplifting, not critical and insulting. Whatever life changing improvements he suggests will be beneficial to you both.

I want you to think of a gift that a friend or a parent gave you. In the beginning, when you first received the gift you treated it with such care and honor. Better yet, leading up to receiving the gift you were on your best behavior so that you can receive what it is you wanted. As mentioned earlier when you meet a man, make sure you are meeting the man and not the façade. Is he really who he represents himself to be? How do you know? Listen to his responses and pay attention to his reactions when he disagrees with you or becomes angry about something you did or are going to do.

For example, do you both share the same values and morals? If not, is he attempting to make you reverse you values in order to fit his? Does he give significance to what's important to you and is this man a good fit for your life? An abusive man's first tool is to strip you of all your resources, family, friends, education, etc. A man that is not abusive will want you to further your education and will value that your family is an important part of your life.

The abuser's plan is to isolate you so that if abuse exists on any level your access to family and friends will be limited. While abuse is occurring in your relationship you are not able to flee to your family as quickly. Another sign to look for are verbal put downs. This might start out really slow in the beginning of an abusive relationship but will gradually become an everyday routine if allowed.

For example, I know a woman who was married for two years and had an abusive husband. While he was physically abusive from time to time most of his abuse was verbal and emotional. If she cooked dinner or breakfast it wasn't good enough. If the wife went shopping, the grocery list was wrong or she didn't purchase the correct supplies for the house. The husband would continue his rants and complaints and began calling his wife names like, stupid, incompetent, etc.

When does complaining turn abusive? The writing is on the wall when a man is constantly putting you down making it verbal abuse. Verbal abuse becomes emotionally draining and therefore discouraging. An abuser hopes to capture the mind first because he knows that once this is accomplished, she will permit him to continue to be abusive causing her to feel hopeless.

Women often ignore the signs of abuse because they are thinking they can change the abusers' behavior. In the midst of a woman waiting for the abuser to change they are beating down their spirit and wasting valuable time of the life God has given them. A woman can recognize signs of a potentially abusive man in the beginning of a relationship if she opens her eyes and chooses not to ignore the signs. A mans character will therefore become his destiny and if you don't want to become part of his abusive destiny then don't ignore the signs.

Physical abuse can be a punch to the face or a slap. Even if a man does not do any of the above things I've mentioned, if a man puts his hands on you in a way that makes you feel uncomfortable, GET OUT! There is no such thing as working it out if a man is abusive. These behaviors do not change and the situations often escalate ending in death or close to it. Sadly, women will stay in a physically violent relationship and often times end up seriously injured or dead.

A woman who wants to leave her abusive man should secretly make a file of his abuse. Take photos of the bruises and injuries. By this stage in the relationship the woman is normally isolated from her family and friends. Therefore tell someone, anyone who will listen. Tell a beautician, mailman, pastor or neighbor. You'd be surprise at who will listen and may already have an idea that you're being abused. They may even refer you to a safe house. This woman should also try telling her family of what is going on and gain as many resources as possible. The next thing you should do is plan your escape and a list of items you are going to need. Furniture and material items can be replaced, your life cannot.

Another thing a woman should do is file a police report in her local police station. It is not enough to file the report, YOU MUST FOLLOW THROUGH, by pressing the necessary charges and file for an order of protection. Understand that if you drop the charges or do not press charges you just became a victim all over again. If you allow fear to consume you then you will never break free of his mental grasp. Furthermore, the abuser is smiling inside because he knows that if you didn't file the charges he still has you.

There are also safe houses for women who are trying to flee abusive relationships. Your local police precinct/station will have a domestic violence officer who can assist you. There are twenty-four hour hotlines to call and programs available to you and your children. You can all be relocated to a safer environment. The website www. ndvh.org offers a lot of valuable information. The National domestic violence hotline is 1-800-799-SAFE.

Don't feel trapped or stuck because the truth of the matter is, you aren't stuck. By regaining your resources and leaving your abuser you are taking your power back. This is not your fault so stop blaming yourself and making excuses for him. If money is an issue there are organizations out there to help you gain the financial means necessary to leave this abusive relationship permanently; such as *Collection of Hope*. This organization provides resources, rent, security, childcare, food and shelter for any woman who wants to escape or is attempting to escape an abusive relationship. Log on to www.justinahmcfadden. com for further information or face book: collection of hopeYou can go from victim to victor if only you know how to regain your power.

Claim your change and cross the intersection to a life of hope. There is a man out there who will love you and treat you in the manner a lady should be treated. I hope this helps you and empowers you to move on to a fulfilling and violence free relationship.

The following are some, not limited to, examples exhibited by a potentially abusive man:

Emotional Abuse:

1 You look fat and I'm embarrassed to be seen with you in public.

2 I know your cheating on me. (Very jealous and possessive)

3 I don't know why you're going to school; it's just a waste of time.

4 Why don't you put me first, before the kids and your family

Verbal Abuse:

1 You can be such a bitch sometimes

2 I can't stand the sight of you, I will ruin you financially.

3 You will never leave me, who would want you anyway?

4 You're a worthless piece of (*profanities…*)

Physical Abuse:

1 Throwing household objects when angry

2 Clinching of fists or holding hand up simulating a slapping motion

3 Punching walls or inanimate objects when having a disagreement

4 Violently grabbing you when trying to walk away

Chapter 6

Why Relationships, Why not remain Single?

I know, I know... why even ask this question right? Well, I recently heard a young lady describe in detail why she feels she needs a man. She listed in the following order the reasons: *Companionship, Entertainment, Intimacy and Transportation.* (CEIT pronounced see it) She said to her girlfriend if you don't see it (CEIT) leave it. Her girlfriend simply laughed and told her, "You have me for companionship, I drive you wherever it is you need to go, you confide in me about everything, and then she asked, "Am I that boring?" As amusing as this story may be, there is some pragmatism to it.

She knew what she wanted and what to look for in a man. If that man couldn't provide what she was looking for she would simply move on until she found someone who could.

What is the point you ask? Sometimes you simply may not be ready for a relationship even when you think you are. The perks or qualities you seek may be possessed by the friends you already have. You may have other obligations that preoccupy you such as school, work, or family. Relationships require time, lots of it. You may not have the time to pursue or become involved with anyone at this point in your life. First and foremost, if you're not happy, how do you expect to make someone else feel happy? Lets face it, people want and need to feel good about themselves before being involved in a productive relationship.

I often tell people that being in a relationship is like a fulltime job. Even when you're apart, you must consider the other person's feelings when making a decision that involves the two of you. I remember coming home from work exhausted and ready to jump in the shower then bed but my girlfriend had other plans. She purchased two tickets to a play and never told me about it until I returned home that evening. She wanted it to be a surprise. So in an effort not to disappoint her or seem unappreciative of her surprise, I simply showered and joined her for the Broadway show. What I'm getting at is this. Although seemingly minor, I made the sacrifice of coming home from work exhausted and just went along with the program.

I recall my neighbor coming to me complaining about his wife not wanting to go to Haiti because the weather was too hot. My neighbor's wife responded, "I would rather go to Puerto Rico." My neighbor Ruben at the time thought it would be a good idea for his children to see their heritage being that he himself was from Port-au-Prince, Haiti. His wife's idea was the same, except she was from Ponce, Puerto Rico.

After long discussions, they both decided that they would make a trip to both islands within the course of the year. In relationships, simply put you must be willing to compromise and make sacrifices often doing things you normally aren't accustomed to doing.

It would be unfair for anyone to get involved with someone they really don't have time for. Sure, many of us enter relationships for the purposes of convenience to begin with but communicate this to him in the beginning.

I'm quite sure you're familiar with the, *"Friends with benefits,"* arrangement. This is a mutually agreed upon arrangement whereas, no strings attached or commitments are promised, the relationship consists of just sex. Now if this is what you seek, then you already know what it is you want out of a relationship making this chapter a moot point. More often then not, either the man or the woman reneges on the agreement. He or she ends up wanting more and resentment is the result because the other doesn't want to further complicate things. At this stage in your relationship, you must ask yourself, "Am I willing and ready to make these compromises and are there goals I need to fulfill before I become seriously involved with him?" If you're not willing to compromise or make these kinds of sacrifices then maybe you're not ready to be in a relationship.

I have met women that feel they absolutely must be with someone for numerous reasons. Perhaps pressure is being felt from the parents, their biological time clock is ticking or they no longer want to be the third wheel when hanging out with other couples. Whatever the reason, society dictates the norm and often attaches a stigma to women who choose to remain single. Men as well enter into relationships for various reasons. It may start off as it being convenient to be in one but often leads to a more committed relationship. Ironically this is not by the man's standard but by the woman he is with because ultimatums are eventually given. Standards are set from the beginning and he knows from the start that he's not going to enjoy the benefits for much longer without being in a more committed relationship.

*DON'T JUST PRESENT
THE PROBLEM.
TRY TO PRESENT A
SOLUTION TO THE
PROBLEM AS WELL...*

I often ask women when they complain about the man they're with, "Have you suggested a solution to the problem?" Majority of the time, I get no response or a deeply contemplated retort. Many women will complain about the man they're with but are not willing to present a solution to the problem. My theory, as mentioned previously, is that you subconsciously decided his behavior or maybe priorities you had in mind did not warrant leaving him. Pros outweighing the cons may be the reason why you haven't decided to take such drastic measures in leaving. You're willing to work it out. But communication is the key because my next question will be, "Does he even know how you feel?" She will usually respond, "Well he should, I complain about it often enough!" I further explain that men do not want to argue so they'll tune you out or simply leave until they feel you've calmed down.

May I suggest an alternative? It would be more productive to discuss your concerns (with a possible solution) while over dinner (preferably outside the house) or during that stroll on the beach. Men are more receptive to what a woman has to say while in a relaxed or tranquil setting. Come across in a suggestive manner and check your emotions at the door. For example, a friend recently confided in me about his extended hours at work taking a toll on his wife and their marriage. Unbeknownst to her, he was working long hours because of deadlines he had to meet and was recently considered for promotion as a result of his hard work. He wanted it to be a surprise but his long hours resulted in her having an attitude every time he came home. I know his wife who happens to be a good friend of the family. He asked that I intervene and explain to her that his profession is very demanding and without the overtime, he wouldn't be able to maintain their current lifestyle. He further explained that every time he tried to tell her so, it would end up in an argument. I agreed and waited for her to bring the subject to my attention during a house warming party. She being very concerned about the fate of their marriage complained that she needed him at home so that he may spend more time with the kids. I asked if she ever mentioned this to him. She excitedly explained, "Off course I do, all the time. I tell him as soon as he walks in that this marriage is not going to last very long if he's not willing to make a change in his work schedule." So when presenting your argument, you threaten to leave him? Do you suggest any solutions to the problem? Becoming a bit uncomfortable, she realized what I was getting at. She realized that every time she bought up the subject, she threatened him with divorce. Never once did she offer or present a solution.

Seemingly unwilling to compromise at first she realized that she approached the situation abruptly and saw from her husband's perspective why he worked the long hours he did. I suggested that she should get a babysitter for the night and invite him out to dinner. Express to him that she is willing to cut back on a few household expenses, maybe downgrade the cable, and trade in the Mercedes for a Nissan until he receives the promotion he is working so diligently for. Also express to him that being home more often will benefit the kids tremendously and will be conducive to having the family structure she so strongly desires.

Needless to say, she took my advice and ended up taking him to a bed & breakfast resort for the weekend. While expressing her concerns in this manner and being in an environment more conducive for repose, he was more receptive and understanding to what she had to say. Being that his commute time was approximately an hour to an hour and a half depending on traffic, he decided to create an office space in their home which enabled him to complete small assignments at home while cutting down on his hours at work. His work hours went from 60-65 hrs to 45-50 hr with weekends off. Attending more soccer and football games, being at his daughter's dance recitals alleviated the tensions that existed at home and saved their marriage. Relationships are compromise and problems will be plentiful when solutions seem far and few in between. But when approached from an empathetic perspective, well thought out plans while presenting a solution on how to improve your current situation will help strengthen any relationship.

Chapter 7

There's No Turning Back from Awareness

You being the well informed woman that you are often fail to use your intuition as your guide. This is especially true when starting out in a relationship with a man you've only known for a few weeks. This doesn't sound like enough time but more often than not, a man reveals much of himself to you during this time. This information is constantly made available to you during the times spent together whether you know it or not. It could be during dinner or just going on a short drive to the movies. If you know what to look for, you will eventually be able to determine if this man is right for you.

During your conversations, watch his body language, hand positions and mannerisms while speaking to him. In casual conversations, he will most likely be relaxed and not reveal much but try to ask more pressing questions. For example, ask about his previous relationships and why they're no longer together if he brings them up voluntarily. Be tactful while doing so. While he's speaking, try not to interrupt because during this time, a man will retrospectively speak of his past while revealing much about himself. Your silence while being attentive will make him feel the need to elaborate. We frequently bring up past relationships and subliminally make comparisons to our current ones without realizing it. Make suggestions as to how you both can solve certain issues that involve your relationship.

While doing this, observe his hand and arm position. Based on past studies involving the human psyche and non verbal communications, it is virtually impossible for anyone to lie if being observed by someone knowledgeable in this field of study. Ask him about his financial goals or what it is he is looking for in a relationship. If you see him cross his arms or he begins to use his hands simulating back off as if he were applying the breaks, he's telling you just that, to back off! You are making him feel uncomfortable and perhaps he is not being totally honest with you. While in conversation with him, ask him about issues that are very important to you and see if he looks away from you, hesitates and comes back with an answer. These gestures (folding his arms, hands with palms facing you etc…) indicate a defensive posture and you've possibly touched on a subject he's really not comfortable in discussing with you. Or maybe he's hiding something and doesn't want to reveal anything too personal about his past. He's not ready to open up to you at this time. As the relationship progresses, he should open up more and feel comfortable about discussing his past. Initially men will not reveal much about their past until they feel confident that they can trust you. This is a defense mechanism that we have because we want to know that you're genuinely interested in us before revealing too much about ourselves. Based on my interviews, I find this to be more evident when a man is really interested and considers being in a more committed relationship with you. He will become a better listener and want to find out ways to please you.

When sitting at the dinner table, see if he places his wine glass or any other obstacle between you two. This often indicates an imaginary barrier of defense that he puts in place. Maybe you touched on something that he's not ready to open up about just yet. For example, I discovered some time ago that I tend to sit or lean back and place my hand on the armrest, head tilted to one side with my elbow projecting outward when disagreeing or strongly considering a topic or subject being discussed. But when I'm receptive to the subject matter being presented, I will lean forward with part of my arms leaning on the table and hands clasped while being more attentive to what's being said. The conversation caused him to place an imaginary barrier between you two. Is he seated in his chair with his feet facing the door? What about his hand and finger position? Are they clasped or folded?

There is a plethora of information out there on how you can read someone's body language in regards to his level of comfort. How one responds while under pressure and to know what to look for, read and interpret what it is you're seeing is an acquired ability. Once you've taken an effort to become more aware of what it is you're seeing, there's no turning back. You took the time out to arm yourself with this knowledge of being able to read a potential mate and start to notice things you've never before noticed. You don't have to be a psychologist to make a determination as to why one positions themselves the way they do to make this work to your advantage. However, I do assure you of one thing, you will never view any conversation the same after knowing what to look for.

Now if he behaves in a way that is inconsistent with how he responds, you know something is up. Whatever it is your asking, causing his arms to fold (defensive position) will and should make you more curious as to why he reacted this way. Perhaps he's hiding something. Or maybe he disagrees with something that was asked or said. This ability to sense when someone's uncomfortable or reactions to what is being said is not only effective in distinguishing between Mr. Right from Mr. Wrong. You can also use these observations during job interviews, with your kids, and colleagues. Knowing how to do this skill also helps to avoid many conflicts with him, friends and family. Have fun with your new ability as it is interesting to see how others convey their thoughts without saying a word.

You becoming a better listener and observer will make you more aware of many potential situations before they come to fruition. This also prevents you from wasting each other's time before it is to late. With being aware of his intentions, you can make an informed decision as to remain or exit the relationship before getting too involved.

Chapter 8

No Excuses, You owe it to yourself

A woman will often stick by their man in various situations. The relationship can be fulfilling or it can sometimes be abusive. I've heard women make excuses for their husbands, fiancés and boyfriends for many reasons. One being, he loves me or he has too many obligations, he's under a lot of stress or he works too many hours to spend the time with me.

Whatever the reason is, you deserve to be in a healthy and fulfilling relationship. I've been guilty of this in the past, often accused of not making enough time or not spending quality time. Many times I would use work as an excuse. I realized more often than not I was just being selfish and felt I had more important things to do. This happens often when a relationship becomes stagnate. You begin to feel as if you have nothing more in common with the person you're with. Feeling bored and unappreciated, it's either time to find a solution or make a change.

You see, no matter how many hours a man works or whatever stress he may be under, if he loves you, you will have that power to alleviate your man's tensions. A man that cares for you and loves you will want to be with you during difficult times. Few if any excuses will be made if he sees how supportive you are. If it's work he's stressed about, he will share that with you. If he has financial concerns he will inform you of such. When a man confides in you about what's weighing heavy on his mind, it's because he trusts you. Way too often, women make excuses as to why their men are distant, confrontational or perhaps even abusive at times. A woman that stays in an abusive relationship has grown very dependent on the man that is abusive to her.

She no longer feels in control and has relinquished her power to a man that wants to control her. I'm not just referring to physical abuse. For abuse comes in many forms. Verbal abuse being as common as emotional abuse or neglect can drive any woman away if she has the strength to leave. Maybe you find yourself staying with him for financial reasons or you desperately want a father figure for your kids or you simply may not want to be alone. If you find yourself in a situation I just described, go back to the reevaluation stage while asking yourself, "Is being unhappy really worth having him pay half my rent?" The kids need a male role model. Is this the role model I want for my kids? I have never been alone but he doesn't respect me. Is staying with him worth my happiness and peace of mind?

If you answered yes to any of the above, chances are you've been making excuses as to why you shouldn't leave. Remember, there are always alternatives to being financial independent, finding a positive role model that not only respects you but is also great with the kids. Perhaps even finding a roommate until your finances become more stable may work to your advantage.

You owe it not only to yourself but to your children because if mom is unhappy, the children will definitely sense this and despise the man you are with. This often leads to conflict forcing the mother to choose between the man and her children. I've seen women make the wrong decision and ultimately end up being miserable. If a man makes you choose between him and the children, he doesn't have your best interest at heart. A woman should never be in this predicament of having to do so but this happens all the time.

Now again, there are exceptions to what I have just outlined. If your children are adults and simply being possessive, you may have to make other arrangements and hopefully the man you are with is patient enough to weather the storm. He may have to convince the rest of your family why it would be beneficial to have him in their lives. I find that being in this situation usually resolves itself when they see how happy the man makes mom. The children will eventually come around and see that her new found love keeps a smile on her face.

Be patient and ask your children to be as well. If he has a strong resolve, he will remain and win the kids over but if he is weak and impatient he will walk. If the latter occurs, be thankful for it was not meant to be. You owe it to yourself to be in a prosperous and healthy relationship no matter the circumstances. Stop making excuses and realize when it is time to move on.

Chapter 9

My Survey...

Over the past three months, I conducted a brief survey and asked men of varying professions, cultures and ethnicities the following two questions:

1. Does it matter if a woman you are interested in has sex with you within 3 days, 3 weeks or 3 months?

2. Would you wait if a woman were to tell you, you have to wait at least 3 months before any physical intimacy (sex) were to take place?

Now keep in my mind, these men that participated in my survey were of multicultural decent and came from all walks of life. These men are doctors, nurses, lawyers, engineers, police officers, construction workers, managers, teachers, business owners and CEOs. I interviewed approximately 100 men and out of the 100, 92 said it wouldn't matter if a woman they were interested in would have sex with them in the aforementioned time. (3 days, 3 weeks or 3 months) In addition, some stated, they would not wait 3 months for a woman to decide if she wanted to be physically intimate with him. One man stated, "Women know within the first or second date if she is willing to have sex with you, so why should I wait 3 months?" Another stated, "If a woman told me that I would have to wait 3 months, I would simply leave because she's using sex for ransom. Its shows a lack of sexual maturity on her part." I know that shouldn't come as a surprise but let me elaborate further on what was said. These men did state that if they were just interested in her physical attributes, a one night stand would be enough for them to lose interest in pursuing anything serious with her.

But if this were a woman of interest, he would pursue her whether it was 3 days, 3 weeks or 3 months. Now out of the 8 remaining, 6 stated that they would wait if there was great distance between them and felt that this would develop into a serious relationship. They would rather not be told by the woman they're courting if a time parameter was imposed when it came to sex. The 2 remaining said they would also wait but would have a SP until the woman that they're truly interested in comes around.

An SP is a side piece. These women have mutually agreed upon *"friends with benefits"* arrangements whereas their relationships only consist of sex and nothing else.

I also took the liberty of asking approximately 50 women if they choose to be intimate with their husbands, boyfriends, or significant others in a relatively short period of time. I asked them if they made or would make the man they're interested in wait 3 months to have sex with them. All of the women said no. Majority of them are in healthy, productive relationships, most are even married. But when asked, they didn't see the sense in making a man they wanted to be with wait 3 months.

So in a nutshell, based on the survey, telling a man to wait for a predetermined period of time to have sex with you is ineffective and a turnoff for most. It is true that you ultimately decide if, when and where you're going to have sex with him. You are in complete control over this while a man interested in you will wait patiently (majority of the time) until you decide, providing you don't tell him he is on a time table. If you opt for the latter, at the very least, keep it to yourself and don't tell the man what your intentions are if you plan on making him wait.

WHEN A MAN LOVES
YOU, HE WILL COME
AND DO THE THINGS
YOU ASK OF HIM,
WHEREAS WHEN
A MAN IS IN LOVE
WITH YOU HE WILL
DO THE THINGS
THAT YOU WOULD
EXPECT OF HIM...

Chapter 10

*To Love or to be in Love,
there is a difference...*

It's 5 AM on a Black Friday and I'm sitting here contemplating whether or not I should be at Macy's looking for that coffee table previously advertised or begin writing this chapter. I opted for the latter. I was very enthusiastic about the material presented to you in this chapter and received much input regarding this subject from many of my friends, family and colleagues alike. Much of this was due to the fact that I experienced this (the difference) during my early to mid 20s. I explain why and how in a moment. When women as well as men are asked the question, "What is the difference between a man loving a woman and a man being in love with a woman?" The responses given always stir up heated discussions and debates.

Interestingly enough, when most of us are asked this question pertaining to whether or not there is a difference between loving and being in love, a perplexed look of uncertainty overcomes the person being asked. Majority of the time, when someone has a definitive answer to what this difference is, either they, themselves have experienced this or someone close to them has. I saved the best (scenario) for last.

So for the ladies out there that have not been subjected to learning this concept the hard way, be thankful because I'm going to give you a scenario that will hopefully be thought provoking enough to help you distinguish the difference.

The Scenario:

It was a warm afternoon during the month of September when Laura met Manny. It was shortly after Labor Day and the first day of class has just ended at a well known CUNY located in Long Island, NY. Manny was on his way home when he heard a knock at the rear of his car as he approached the stop sign. The young lady named Laura looked as if she were lost. This was not uncommon for newly matriculated students arriving for the first time. As Manny rolled down the window to inquire as to what the urgency was, she quickly announced that she missed the bus and wanted to know if Manny could drop her off at the nearest bus station. Manny agreed as she entered his car.

"So what's your name?" Manny asked as they proceeded outside the lot. "Laura", she responded. "Do you live in the area?" Manny inquired. "Yes, as a matter of fact I do. Not to far from here." Laura said with a smile. "Well maybe I can drop you off because the bus schedule is slow today", offered Manny. Laura politely accepted and they were on their way.

During their commute, the dialogue made Laura feel as if they had much in common. Prior to her departure the two exchanged numbers and Laura agreed to remain in contact with Manny. Several months passed and they spent a lot of time discussing future endeavors, family and school. Within that year, Manny and Laura became an item and the subject of marriage was a frequent topic of conversation. It was approximately ten months when they decided to be engaged and then married. Laura felt extremely compatible with Manny and very comfortable around his family. But at times, Laura felt something was missing. She couldn't quite put her finger on it but she knew the feeling of uncertainty was starting to get the best of her.

Manny had a lot to offer and with a stable career as an ECT (Electronic Computer Technician). Laura knew he would be a good provider but something was amiss. Laura knew she cared for him and loved him but simply wasn't in love with him. Laura, based on the love stories she has read and her girlfriends' accounts on the feelings they had once she fell in love wasn't experiencing any of these emotions.

"Maya, when you and Reynolds tied the knot, how did you know he was the one?" Laura asked of her best friend. "Well you know what you know and feel what you feel", answered Maya. "Come on Maya, stop speaking in riddles and tell me what it was you felt and knew that made you marry him", Laura retorted. "Well you feel certain emotions when you fall in love." "Meaning", Laura becoming more attentive and even more curious as to what Maya meant. Maya began to explain sensing Laura's eagerness to learn. "I felt butterflies in my stomach just with the anticipation of seeing him. Not only did I look forward to being with him, I always wanted to find out what it is he enjoys. Whether it was a shirt I saw him express interest in or the foods he likes to eat, I found the need to please him and enjoyed doing it as long as Reynolds and I were together. I would take special interest in whatever it was he enjoyed doing. Sometimes I would feel nervous around him and would wonder what he was thinking while being with him." Maya finding herself becoming nostalgic began to reminisce about the beginning stages of their relationship.

Although Laura and Manny were together for three years, she knew something was missing and did not want to hurt him. At the conclusion of their conversation, Maya gave her girlfriend sound advice. "If you don't feel that you're in love with him, you have to let him know before it's too late." It hurts more to tell someone this several years later as opposed to letting them know in the beginning stages of a relationship.

The Lesson:

Maya was right. It wouldn't be fair to be with someone for a long period of time if you know you are not in love with him. And marrying the guy just makes it worse while adding on to the hurt and pain even more so when you decide to end it. I've heard of people being married for ten, eleven, even twelve years only to find out by their wife/husband that they were never in love with that person. They claimed to have remained in the relationship because of the children or some other reason. More often than not, people stay in a loveless marriage because of complacency and it is simply too much of an inconvenience for them to go back out there and make another attempt at finding real love.

Marriage, I often hear is now considered and often referred to as a business relationship. Financial gurus even advise that a married couple should never commingle all of their earnings because of what may come. Why do you think prenuptials are such in demand and becoming increasingly popular? The criteria of being rich or well off no longer applies to couples wanting a prenuptial. They often advise couples to have separate accounts while keeping one joint account for common household expenses. You can't help but to wonder, with advice like this, why even bother getting married? It seems as if we're being told to prepare for the worse. But the truth of the matter is more often then not, people get married for all the wrong reasons and end up in divorce. Far too often they realize years into the relationship that they remained married for selfish reasons and end up hurting the person they are married to. Unfortunately being in love wasn't one of them. But often couples think that they would grow to fall in love with their spouse or figured they would eventually grow on them.

I asked a good friend of my many years ago as he spoke about getting an anniversary gift for his wife, "Byron, how do you know when you're in love?" He pondered the question and explained to me the following. "You know when you're in love when the woman you're with is someone you think about day and night. You think of ways to make her happy and do things that you wouldn't ordinarily do for any other woman. Like for example, you may come over and do her laundry for her or fix things around the house, maybe even learn how to dance even though you know you have two left feet. Why? Because you know that this is what will make her happy. Or you may see a yellow school bus passing by and say to yourself, that's my baby's favorite color. I'll get her some yellow roses on the way home from work."

Being young, I thought his descriptive account of how it feels to be in love was merely infatuation and nothing else. Unbeknownst to me, I was in for a rude awakening. At the time I asked Byron this question, I was with someone I thought I may have possibly been in love with. But with Byron being married, I figured I could get a more definitive answer because I knew he deeply cared for his wife. I also knew that he was in love with his wife of only a couple of years. He explained how he felt similar to what Maya revealed to Laura in the previous scenario. He would feel tingling sensations in his stomach just before seeing her and would always talk about what restaurant he wanted to take her to. It seemed as if all of his plans included her.

At the time I was in a relationship and thought I was falling in love but retrospectively speaking I was on the rebound. I mean I loved and cared for the woman I was with but found doing things for her was often arduous and time consuming. I was not in love but knew that I cared enough to try and work at it. I didn't feel these sensations or experience any of the emotions described by either Maya or Byron.

I was under the preconceived notion that I would eventually grow to fall in love with her and experience these feelings of love. But to no avail these feelings never came.

You see, loving someone and being in love with someone has a huge distinction. *When a man loves you, he will come and do the things you ask of him, whereas when a man is in love with you he will do the things that you would expect of him.* Do you see the difference now? I'll give you an example. Recently I asked a Paramedic by the name of Shauna what she thought was the difference between being loved and being in love. She gave an interesting account of her own experience.

Shauna loves to ride her new motorcycle and was stuck one summer afternoon while riding in the rain. Being a newly licensed and relatively inexperienced biker when it came to riding in the rain, she quickly pulled under a nearby tunnel for shelter. She pulled out her cell phone and called her boyfriend for assistance. Not only did he seem unwilling to help, he was very dismissive and told her to wait the rain out. Shauna knew that if she asked him to come, he would've. But felt she shouldn't have to beg him for help. Now her boyfriend lived approximately ten minutes from where she was stuck at the time. He was at home and really couldn't be bothered. Needless to say, she simply did just that and waited about one half hour for the rain to cease and continued on her way. This she explained was an eye opener for her and realized at that very moment, this wasn't the man for her. This coupled with the many other incidents involving her requests for assistance or supportiveness began to weigh heavy on her mind.

Several months later Shauna met someone during a call she received while on duty. He was a physician's assistant by the name of Paul and the two started a relationship. Shauna recently moved into her new apartment and had some plumbing issues. Her sink was leaking and would create a small puddle just outside her kitchen sink. It only took one time for Shauna to express her concern regarding the leak prompting Paul to show up at her apartment. Paul came after work with tool box in hand and a Plumbing book in the other. *Although Paul knew nothing about plumbing he did what was expected of him.* Shauna did not have to beg or plead with him in anyway nor did she ask for his assistance.

I find that men for the most part will do what is asked of them. Even if they have a busy schedule or work many hours but often with reluctance viewing her requests as tasks. This is because he cares for you or loves you and/or the relationship is based on convenience. But a man that is in love will voluntarily come to your rescue without being asked because he doesn't want to see you, the woman he is in love with endure any hardships. A man in love with you is your protector and wants to make you feel secure in the relationship. He doesn't want you to turn to anyone else for assistance in the time of need and will be willing to drop whatever it is he is doing to get to you.

*A MAN WILL BE
INFATUATED AND
THINK HE IS IN LOVE,
WHEREAS A WOMAN
WILL THINK SHE IS
INFATUATED WHEN SHE
IS FALLING IN LOVE.*

So now you know what the difference is. Some of you may be thinking about previous or even current relationships and with clarity what it is he was/is feeling. This all goes under the observation phase during a relationship. Knowing how to determine this (does he love you or is he in love with you) will be an important tool to ascertaining whether or not he is right for you. When a man is in love and feels he has found the right woman, he will help to achieve her goals and expect that woman to reciprocate the same encouragement as well. You both will combine your resources and do whatever it takes to make it happen.

A man that loves you or is in love with you will instinctively want to protect you. He will defend you with his words, actions and overall demeanor if he feels someone or something has the potential to harm you. This will be evident in everything he does while in his absence or presence. For example, if you expressed to him that your male supervisor has been making inappropriate comments, he will make it his business to show up at your job and pick you up after work. The purpose is to show your supervisor and colleagues alike that you have a man and you are not alone. He will patiently wait in the car until you leave your office and get out to open the door for you. If his (her male supervisor) behavior persists, he may have to have a little talk with him.

Or maybe your walk from the train station the other night was a little uncomfortable because of how dark the side streets were. Once you express this to the man that is *in love with you*, he will be waiting for you at the train station every night to drive you home. However a man that *loves you* will call you a cab or maybe suggest taking a more lighted path on the way home. He will probably call you to ensure that you reached home safely but his actions will be slightly different from a man that is in love you.

A Little Q & A Session

I've been with my current boyfriend for a little over a year now. Why hasn't he introduced me to his parents?

AW: He's definitely hiding something. More importantly he's hiding you. There is something or someone he doesn't want you to know about. Reading chapter 4 *The Writing is on the Wall* may help shed some light on why he may be hiding you.

I've been with my boyfriend for three years now. How do I get him to propose to me?

AW: Did you explain to him during the course of your relationship that you eventually wanted to get married? If so, what was his response? If you expressed this to him in the past, and he still hasn't proposed, he may not have any intentions on getting married and has grown complacent in the relationship. You must decide if you want to remain in this relationship unmarried or ask him to make a decision. If you decide on the latter, make sure you stay on top of it or he will never take what you say seriously.

I've been seeing this guy on and off for about six months now. I want more of a commitment but he's back and forth as to whether or not he's ready for a commitment. What should I do?

AW: Well you did mention that you guys were on and off. You can't expect a commitment from a man that you see on and off. This sounds like *"a friends with benefits"* arrangement. Commitments come from being in stable relationships. You may want to reconsider who you want to be in a committed relationship with.

Lately, while being in public with my boyfriend, I catch him staring at other women. Could this be a sign he's losing interest?

AW: No, not necessarily. Did he do this from the beginning of your relationship? Or is this a recent change in his behavior? You should let him know that it bothers you when he does this. A man can admire another woman but if he does so in a disrespectful manner, you can't help but to wonder what he does when your not around. Men are superficial and are going to look at other women. But this doesn't necessarily mean that he's losing interest. Do the things you did in the beginning that attracted him to you in the first place if you feel you need to rekindle that spark.

How do I keep the fire alive in my two year relationship?

AW: Do the things you did when you first started dating him. If its lingerie he likes, surprise him one day after he comes home from work with his favorite negligee. Make it romantic and light some candles. Maybe a change in venue would set the mood. A romantic dinner at your favorite restaurant for just the two of you would be nice if this was something you often did in the beginning. Make love to him in a place he would never expect. Be more spontaneous and more attentive by asking how his day at work was.

I have a good man for the most part. However, when he becomes upset at me, he can be very aggressive with his words. Is this a sign of abuse?

AW: Yes, if what he says hurts and is disrespectful. Abuse comes in mainly three forms: Emotional, Verbal and Physical. This would be considered verbal abuse. If you feel his language is abusive, he may be a potentially abusive man. No relationship should consist of either one of you living in fear. Read chapter 5 (Recognizing the Signs) for examples on the different forms of abuse.

I love my boyfriend. But the only issue I have is he's a momma's boy. If I suggest something, he always runs to his mother for approval. Its really beginning to take a toll on our relationship. Any advice?

AW: Aren't you happy you're not married to him? The good news is this. If it bothers you and you've discuss this with him resulting in no changes being made, move on. Unless of course, you're willing to tolerate this behavior. Momma's boys usually don't change overnight. Good luck with this one.

I've been dating this guy for about a year now and he wants to have sex without a condom. I'm totally against the idea but he won't give in. Any suggestions?

AW: I'm reading how you referred to him as (*this guy*). Seems to be an underlining issue involving trust or perhaps even loyalty. If he can not respect the fact that you prefer to practice safe sex, then he definitely doesn't have your best interest at heart.

I recently developed a crush on my professor. I'm attracted to him but I already have a boyfriend. Since my crush, my feelings for my boyfriend have changed somewhat. Why do I feel guilty?

AW: First off, you shouldn't feel guilty because of a little crush. There's nothing wrong with finding someone else attractive. The problem starts when you act upon these feelings and cheat on the person you're with. If it's just a crush you have, you will probably soon get over it and laugh about it later on with your boyfriend. It is common to see someone as being attractive and comparing him to your current boyfriend. However, if this crush develops into something more intense, maybe you should reevaluate why you are with this guy to begin with.

My boyfriend is African American and I'm Caucasian. His family seems nice but aren't exactly pleased with his decision to be with me. My family disagrees with our relationship as well. Stuck between a rock and a hard place. What should I do?

AW: You will never be content if you live to please others. If you love him and want to be with him, that's all that matters. In a respectful manner, let your family know that you've made a decision to be with him. Either accept it or don't. If they choose the latter, do what makes you happy. Supportive family members may not allows agree with our choices but will come around eventually. I've made decisions that were considered controversial by my family but had a purpose in doing so. Once revealed, my family members were more receptive and understanding in my decision making abilities.

Why am I always attracted to men that are unavailable?

AW: It's human nature to want to take on a challenge every once in a while. You just have to be cautious not to take on the wrong challenges. Pursuing a married man... not a good idea unless you want drama. Besides, think of it this way, how would you feel if someone chased after the man you loved or were with? The same pain that will be caused to another by pursuing their husband will only be reciprocated. It doesn't feel very nice when the shoes on the other foot. There are plenty of eligible bachelors out there waiting for you. Try meeting some.

SOON TO COME BY THE AUTHOR...

OUR QUEST FOR GREATNESS...
WHAT ARE YOU WILLING TO SACRIFICE TO ACHIEVE IT?

YEAR 2010

www.ingramcontent.com/pod-product-compliance
Lightning Source LLC
Chambersburg PA
CBHW051448280526
45785CB00003B/1482